WHODUNNIT?

Narinder Dhami

Paula Zorite

Collins

Contents

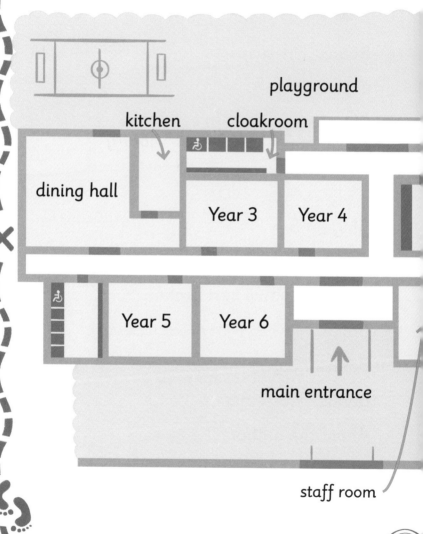

playground

kitchen

cloakroom

dining hall

Year 3

Year 4

Year 5

Year 6

main entrance

staff room

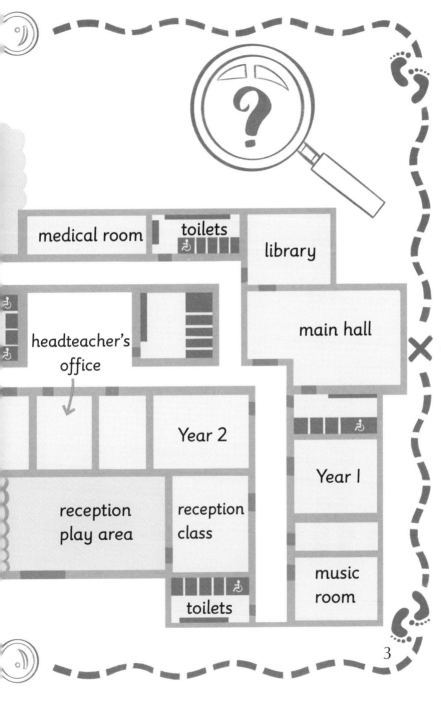

medical room

toilets

library

headteacher's office

main hall

Year 2

Year 1

reception play area

reception class

music room

toilets

3

THE SUSPECTS

Name: Harry Lewis
Height: 118 cm
Successful pranks this term: 4
Detentions: 1
Cheekiness: 15
Detective skills: 25
Prank rating: 27/30

Name: Krish Patel
Height: 124.5 cm
Successful pranks this term: 9
Detentions: 11
Cheekiness: 30
Detective skills: 15
Prank rating: 26/30

Name: Nazreen Ali
Height: 123 cm
Successful pranks this term: 6
Detentions: 2
Cheekiness: 17
Detective skills: 28
Prank rating: 29/30

Name: Lily Chung
Height: 121 cm
Successful pranks this term: 7
Detentions: 4
Cheekiness: 18
Detective skills: 30
Prank rating: 26/30

Chapter 1

"Now, I want you to tell me the truth," Ms Gray said sternly. She looked hard at Harry, Nazreen, Krish and Lily. "Have you been playing one of your jokes in school today?"

The four friends glanced at each other. They all looked puzzled. "No, Ms Gray," they said together.

"We haven't played jokes on anyone for a long time, Ms Gray," Lily added.

"Lily's right," Harry said. "It's been at *least* two days."

"Yes, we put a fake spider in the bottom of Mrs Penny's coffee cup," said Nazreen.

The four of them started giggling.

Ms Gray sighed loudly. "This morning someone made an awful mess in the play space outside the reception classroom," she explained.
"The books were upside-down on the shelves.
The cuddly toys were all over the floor.
There was modelling clay stuck to the carpet.
There was sand in the water tray and water in the sand box."

"Isn't that just a normal day in reception class?" Krish asked.

Ms Gray almost smiled. Then she bit her lip and looked very serious again.

"This is much, much worse," she said.
"The cleaners didn't report it last night, so
I think it must have happened before school
started this morning. Now, be honest with me.
Was this one of your pranks?"

"No, Miss," Harry said quickly. "We wouldn't
trash the play space."

"We wouldn't be mean to the little kids," Nazreen added. "We don't play mean jokes."

"If we *had* done it, we'd have made it *really* funny," said Krish.

"Shush, Krish!" Lily said crossly. She stuck her elbow in his ribs.

"Ow!" Krish gasped.

Ms Gray glared at the four friends. "I intend to investigate this very serious matter and find out exactly who's behind it," she said. "I'll speak to you again after breaktime."

"But it *wasn't* us, Miss," Harry insisted.

"We don't tell lies, Ms Gray," said Nazreen.

"We *always* own up," Krish said.

"We'd confess if we'd done it," said Lily.

Ms Gray didn't look convinced at all.
"If I find out it *was* you, then you will stay
in at lunchtime today to clean up the mess,"
she continued seriously. "You will also be
in detention every lunchtime for the next
two weeks. Is that clear?"

"Yes, Ms Gray," the four friends replied.

Harry, Nazreen, Krish and Lily trudged out of Ms Gray's office. Gloomily, they headed back to their Year Two classroom.

"I suppose Ms Gray will tell our teacher," Nazreen said. "Mrs Penny will be *really* annoyed that we're in trouble again."

"This is so unfair, guys!" Krish complained. "We always get blamed when someone plays a trick."

"Well, we play more tricks than anyone else!"
Lily pointed out.

"Yes, but it's still not fair," Krish muttered.

"Ms Gray says she's going to investigate,"
Harry said. "So, she might find out who really
did it."

"What if she can't find out?" Krish said.
"We'll still get the blame!"

"But we've told Ms Gray it wasn't us," Lily said.
"What else can we do?"

Nazreen sighed and rolled her eyes.
"It's obvious, isn't it?" she said. "We have to —"

Just then, the bell began to ring loudly
for breaktime.

Krish, Harry and Lily couldn't hear a word
Nazreen was saying.

Chapter 2

The bell stopped ringing. Children began rushing out of the classrooms towards the playground.

"That's a brilliant idea, Nazreen," said Harry.

"I know!" Nazreen said. "But we don't have time to hang around. The clock is ticking!"

"Don't panic, guys," said Krish. "We can do this! But where do we start?"

"We do what any detective would do," Lily replied. "First, we visit the scene of the crime!"

The corridors were empty now because all the children were outside. Harry, Nazreen, Krish and Lily hurried through the school to the play space. They kept a sharp eye out for any teachers along the way.

"We'll get into trouble being inside at breaktime," Harry fretted.

"We're in enough trouble already," Nazreen said. "A bit more won't matter!"

The play space was at the end of the corridor, outside the reception classroom.

Nazreen led the way. She turned the corner
of the corridor and stopped dead in shock.
Harry, Krish and Lily bumped into the back
of her.

"Oh dear!" Nazreen said. "This is REALLY bad."

The play space was in a terrible state.
The bookshelves were a mess. The cuddly toys lay around in heaps. There was yellow sand, puddles of water and blobs of modelling clay on the floor.

"I'm not surprised Ms Gray was so angry," Lily said.

"Let's look around," said Harry. "We might find some clues."

"Good idea," Krish agreed. He rushed forward eagerly and tripped over a cuddly penguin lying on the floor. The others sniggered.

It was hard work looking for clues in all the mess. At first, they didn't find anything. But then Krish spotted something half-hidden under a pile of books.

"What's that?" he asked. "It looks like a book bag."

"If it's a book bag, it'll have a name on it," said Harry.

"That will be a brilliant clue!" Nazreen said excitedly.

Krish pulled the book bag out. He looked at the name on the front.

"*Nazreen?*" Krish said. He looked shocked.

Nazreen blushed. "I lost my book
bag yesterday," she said quickly.
"Don't you remember?"

"But what's it doing *here*?" Harry asked, staring
at her suspiciously.

"Did *you* trash the play space for
a joke, Nazreen?" Lily wanted to know.

"Of course not!" Nazreen replied.

"Oh, I guess it's not a real clue then,"
Lily sighed. As she turned away, her foot
slipped on something. She stumbled and let out
a loud scream.

"SSSH!" Harry, Nazreen and Krish said together.

"Sorry, guys," Lily said. "But I think I've found a clue." She bent down to pick up a banana skin from the floor.

Krish frowned. "A banana skin?" he said. "That's a clue?"

"Look, there's an empty box of raisins as well," Nazreen pointed out.

"*And* a cereal bar wrapper," Harry added. "The school tuck shop sells all these things."

"Maybe the person who made the mess left them behind," Lily said. "Let's go to the tuck shop. We can ask who they sold them to."

"Great idea!" Krish said. He turned to leave and tripped over the cuddly penguin again. The others had to clap their hands over their mouths to stifle their laughter.

The four friends dashed off down the corridor towards the playground as fast as they could. Suddenly, they heard footsteps coming towards them.

Chapter 3

Harry and Lily dived behind a tall bookcase.
Nazreen ducked into the cloakroom.
For a moment, Krish was frozen to the spot
in panic. Then he crawled underneath a table.

A few seconds later, Mr Rose hurried along
the corridor. He was the reception class teacher.
Harry, Nazreen, Krish and Lily all liked Mr Rose
very much. He had been their class teacher
when they first started school a few years ago.

Mr Rose was carrying a pile of books. His car keys were on top of the books, but suddenly they slid off onto the floor. Mr Rose put the books on the table. Then he bent down to pick up his keys. To his surprise, he came face to face with Krish.

"Oh, hello, Sir," Krish said awkwardly.

Mr Rose was astonished. "Hello, Krish," he replied. "What are you doing under there?"

Krish climbed out from under the table. "I was hiding, Sir," he explained.

Mr Rose glanced around. "Then I guess Harry, Nazreen and Lily are here somewhere, too?" he said. "You four are always together."

Harry and Lily shuffled out from
behind the bookcase. Nazreen sidled
out of the cloakroom. They all looked
very embarrassed.

"You should be outside in the playground,"
Mr Rose said. He yawned several times and
rubbed his eyes. "Go on. I haven't seen you."

"Are you OK, Sir?" Nazreen asked.
Mr Rose's hair was sticking up as if he
hadn't combed it. His eyes were red-rimmed.
He looked exhausted.

"How's your new baby, Sir?" Krish said.
They all knew Mr Rose and his wife had just
had a baby daughter.

Mr Rose beamed. "She's lovely, thank you,"
he said. "She wasn't well yesterday though, and
we didn't get much sleep. That's why I'm late to
school this morning. I've only just arrived."

He smothered another yawn. "Now get out of here before I change my mind and give you detention."

Harry, Nazreen, Krish and Lily shot off down the corridor and into the playground.

"Now we only have nine minutes of breaktime left!" Harry gasped.

The four friends dashed across the infants' playground to the tuck shop. The shop was in the juniors' part of the playground. An older student, Akbar, was serving the customers.

At once, Krish elbowed his way to the front of the queue. Akbar glared at him.

"Please join the queue and wait your turn," Akbar said firmly.

"But this is an emergency!" Krish said. Akbar ignored him. Harry, Nazreen and Lily hustled Krish away.

"Don't argue with Akbar," Harry whispered. "You know he acts like he's the king of the tuck shop!"

The four friends joined the line of customers. It seemed to take ages. But at last, they reached the head of the queue.

"We only have seven minutes of breaktime left!" Krish wailed.

"What can I get you?" Akbar asked.

"Nothing," Nazreen said. "We just want to ask you something."

"I don't have time to chat," Akbar said. "I'm too busy serving customers."

"But there's no one else behind us," Harry pointed out. "We're the last ones!"

"Well, I have to tidy the tuck shop before breaktime ends," Akbar replied. "This is a very responsible job, you know."

"We're trying to find out who got a banana, raisins and a cereal bar," Lily explained. "Do you remember?"

35

Chapter 4

Harry, Nazreen and Lily stared suspiciously at Krish.

"So it *was* you who trashed the play space!" Harry said.

"No, it wasn't!" Krish cried. "I wouldn't do something so mean. I can't be the *only* person who got those snacks!"

Akbar opened his notebook. "I've sold 15 bananas this week so far," he announced, looking at the totals. "Ten boxes of raisins and 14 cereal bars."

"You see?" Krish said. "There are lots of other suspects!"

"So, they aren't real clues at all," Nazreen said.

"That means we're right back where we started," Lily sighed.

"And there's only six minutes of breaktime left,"
Harry added gloomily. He shoved his hands
into his pockets, and some yellow sand fell out.
The others stared at him in amazement.

"Why have you got sand from the play space
in your pockets, Harry?" Nazreen demanded.

"Was it *you* who made the mess?" Lily asked. "Is *that* how the sand got into your pockets?"

"Tell us the truth, Harry," Krish said.

"No, it *wasn't* me!" Harry replied indignantly.

"So why have you got sand in your pockets?" Lily wanted to know.

Harry looked guilty. "I took it to play a trick on Krish," he muttered. "I was going to put sand in his shoes when we did PE."

"What?!" Krish gasped.

"I thought it would be funny," Harry said.

Krish grinned. "Yes, it *would* have been funny, to be fair!" he agreed.

"I'm starting to get a bit fed up with all these tricks," Nazreen said. "I can understand why Ms Gray is annoyed with us."

"And we've just wasted another minute," Lily pointed out. "There's only five minutes of breaktime left now."

"I've got an idea," Krish said. "Why don't we ask the reception kids if they saw anything suspicious this morning?"

"You mean, we might find a witness?" Nazreen said. "Krish, you're a genius!"

The four of them dashed from the juniors' playground back to the infants'. There they found a big group of the younger children playing together.

Krish waded right into the middle of the group. "STOP!" he yelled. "We need to talk to you!"

The young children froze on the spot. They all looked very frightened. Two of them burst into tears.

"Are we in trouble?" a little boy asked.

Nazreen rolled her eyes. "Forget what I just said about Krish being a genius!" she muttered to Lily and Harry. Then she smiled at the little boy. "No, you're not in trouble," Nazreen told him. "We just want to ask you all something."

"Is it a game?" the little boy asked.

"Yes, it's a game," Harry said. "It's called *Can You Remember?*"

The young children clapped their hands and looked excited.

"So, can you remember who came to your classroom this morning?" Lily asked.

The reception children glanced at each other.

"We had a different teacher because Mr Rose was late," one of them said.

"Did you see anyone else?" asked Krish.

All the young children shook their heads.
But then the little boy gave a gasp.

"Yes, I *did* see someone else!" he cried.

Harry, Nazreen, Krish and Lily glanced at each other in excitement.

"Who?" Lily asked.

"It was that girl from Year Six," the little boy said. "The one who wears the big, sparkly hairslides!"

"Oh no! Not Year Six Mary!" said Krish

Chapter 5

"Did I win the game?" the little boy asked.

Harry, Nazreen, Krish and Lily didn't reply. They stood staring at each other in dismay. The infant school children were secretly a little scared of the Year Six pupils. Harry, Nazreen, Krish and Lily didn't have much to do with them at all.

Krish gulped. "We'll have to go and talk to her," he said.

"We'd better go right away before we change our minds," Nazreen said.

The four of them turned and headed back to the juniors' part of the playground.

"Maybe Mary's had to go home," Harry said hopefully.

"Maybe she's ill," Nazreen said.

"Or maybe she's left to go to the dentist," Krish suggested.

"No, there she is!" Lily said.

Mary was sitting on the playground wall, with friends. She was reading a magazine.

"Go on, Harry," Krish said persuasively. "Go and ask Mary if *she* trashed the play space."

Harry looked very worried. "Why me?" he said. "What about Nazreen?"

"Why *me?*" Nazreen said. "Why can't Lily do it?"

"I think Krish should do it," Lily said.

"So do I," said Harry.

"Me, too," said Nazreen. "Go on, Krish."

The four of them shuffled nervously over to Mary. Harry, Nazreen and Lily hung back a little and pushed Krish towards her.

"Hi, Mary," Krish said in a very polite voice. "Can I ask you something?"

Mary shrugged and put her magazine down. "Sure," she said. "But make it quick."

"Did you go to the reception classroom this morning?" Krish asked.

Mary nodded. "I took a message for Mr Rose from my teacher," she said. "But Mr Rose wasn't there. I saw the trashed play space, though. It was *terrible*. Mr Rose was supposed to clear it up yesterday afternoon, but he didn't."

"It wasn't *you* who messed up the play space, was it?" Krish blurted out.

Mary glared at him. "No, it wasn't!"
she snapped.

"Did you see anyone else there this morning?"
Nazreen asked bravely.

"Yep," said Mary. "I saw your friend."
She pointed at Lily. "She was hanging around
the play space. I don't know what she was
up to."

Harry, Nazreen and Krish all spun around to stare at Lily. Lily flushed bright pink and bit her lip.

"Did *you* trash the play space, Lily?" Krish asked.

"Of course not," Lily replied. "I went there to hide Nazreen's book bag for a joke!"

Nazreen groaned. "Another joke!" she sighed.

The four of them began to walk back to the infants' playground.

"We only have two minutes of breaktime left," Harry said gloomily. "And we *still* have no idea who messed up the play space."

Suddenly Lily stopped dead. "Oh!" she
said breathlessly. "Remember what Mary said?"

Lily turned and ran back towards Mary.
Puzzled, Harry, Nazreen and Krish followed her.

"Mary!" Lily yelled at the top of her voice.

Mary almost jumped out of her skin.
"What now?" she snapped.

"You said something about Mr Rose,"
Lily panted. "You said he was *supposed* to clear
up the play space *yesterday afternoon*?"

Mary nodded. "My mum's one of the school cleaners," she explained. "She told me Mr Rose couldn't find his car keys yesterday after school. He turned the play space upside-down looking for them. Mr Rose felt bad he'd made such a mess. He told the cleaners that *he'd* tidy it up."

"It was *Mr Rose* all along?" gasped Nazreen.

Chapter 6

The bell rang for the end of breaktime.
Krish was looking a little confused.

"So *Mr Rose* trashed the play space?" he asked.

"Yes, but only because he was looking for his
car keys," Harry said.

"And he said he'd tidy up so the cleaners didn't
have to do it," Lily added.

Krish looked even more puzzled. "But he didn't
tidy up, did he?" he pointed out.

"No," said Nazreen. "I wonder why he didn't?"

"Maybe it was something to do with his baby being sick," Lily suggested.

They went inside the school.

"So, are we going to tell Ms Gray?" said Harry.

Krish frowned. "Will Mr Rose get into trouble?" he asked.

"But if we don't tell Ms Gray, then *we'll* get into trouble!" Lily pointed out.

The four of them stopped outside their classroom and stared at each other.
They weren't quite sure what to do.

"Oh, there you are," Ms Gray called. She was walking down the corridor towards them.
She looked very serious. "I want to speak to you before you go to class."

Harry, Nazreen, Krish and Lily followed Ms Gray into her office. None of them really knew what they were going to say to her.

"It wasn't us who trashed the play space, Miss," Krish burst out. "Honest!"

"But we'd like to help clear it up," Lily said.

"We'll give up our lunchtime to help," Harry offered.

"We'll work really hard to get it looking nice again," said Nazreen.

Ms Gray smiled. "I know now that you aren't to blame," she said. "Mr Rose told me he made the mess yesterday. He was searching for his lost car keys. But then he had to rush off home suddenly because his wife called to say their baby was ill. So, he didn't have time to tidy up."

Now Harry, Nazreen, Krish and Lily understood exactly what had happened.

"I think Mr Rose would be very grateful for help to tidy up the play space," said Ms Gray. "He's rather exhausted at the moment because of the baby."

"We'd love to help Mr Rose," Harry said eagerly.

"We're fed up with jokes now, Ms Gray," Nazreen said. "We're tired of getting blamed for everything."

"Especially things we haven't done!" said Krish.

"We're not going to play any more jokes from now on, Ms Gray," Lily said.

Ms Gray looked pleased. "I'm very glad to hear it," she said.

Outside Ms Gray's office, Krish turned to Nazreen. "Did you mean what you said to Ms Gray, Naz?" he asked. "Are you really fed up with playing jokes?"

Nazreen nodded. "Jokes are for kids,"
she replied. "We're growing up now. We'll be in
Year Three soon!"

"That's a shame," Krish replied.

They went down the corridor towards the Year
Two classroom. Suddenly, they heard a scream
from behind them.

"What was that?" Lily gasped, spinning around.

"I think it came from Ms Gray's office!"
said Harry.

Nazreen looked sternly at Krish. His face
looked a little guilty.

"What *have* you done, Krish?" Nazreen asked.

"I found a toy snake in the play space," Krish explained. "I was going to hide it in Lily's backpack. But I put it under Ms Gray's desk instead when I was pretending to tie my shoelaces."

Harry and Lily burst out laughing.

"Well, I guess we're not in Year Three yet!" Nazreen said. And she laughed, too.

TOP FIVE BEST PRANKS

I. My best-ever joke was when I hid a big fake bug in the fruit bowl at the tuck shop!

2. It was so funny when I turned Lily's book bag inside-out! I emptied the bag, turned it inside-out, put everything back and zipped it up again. She couldn't work out what had happened!

3. I loved it when the four of us pretended we'd cracked our tablet screens! Our teacher Mrs Penny was very annoyed with us. But it was just a screensaver!

4. I offered Mr Rose one of my joke sweets. It was really salty. His face was so funny!

5. I couldn't stop laughing last week! Mrs Penny was ill, and we had a new teacher. We kept switching names when he asked. The new teacher was so confused!

Yes, it was *so* funny!

HOW TO BE A GREAT DETECTIVE!

Detectives have many different skills.

- They know how to look for different clues at the scene of a crime.

- They must be observant and notice when things don't seem right or look out of place.

◔ They must be good at interviewing witnesses and working out who is telling the truth.

◔ They must keep an open mind about the evidence and not jump to conclusions.

Do you think you could be a great detective? Try the following activities to test your detecting skills!

FINGERPRINTS

Crime scenes are always checked for fingerprints.

Fingerprints are unique, so a detective can match fingerprints to a suspect. Fingerprints are made of eight different pattern shapes, like loops and arches in billions of different combinations.

Did you know: even identical twins don't have the same fingerprints!

Can you match Harry's fingerprint to one of the four different fingerprints below?

Harry's fingerprint

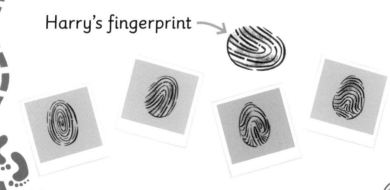

Use an inkpad or paint on one of your fingertips. Press your finger carefully on a piece of white paper.

FOOTPRINTS

Crime scenes are always searched for footprints.

Detectives can often tell what brand and size of shoes or trainers the suspect was wearing.

Sometimes the footprint can help work out the height and shape of a suspect.

Shoe prints are slightly different because of the way you walk so even if you have the same trainers you won't have the same shoe print!

Can you match Krish's shoe print to the four patterns below?

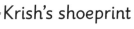
Krish's shoeprint

About the author

A bit about me …

My name's Narinder and I was born near Birmingham. My dad is Indian and my mum is English.

Narinder Dhami

Why did you want to be an author?

I've always enjoyed reading other people's stories. I was the kid who always had a pile of books to read and two or three books on the go at the same time. I never really thought about why I wanted to be an author. It just happened, but it felt very right.

How did you get into writing?

I used to be a primary school teacher, and I was in charge of purchasing books. I remember thinking that I could write a better story than some of the books I saw. So I did!

What is it like for you to write?

I go into a different world inside my head.

What is a book you remember loving reading when you were young?

I loved the Pookie books when I was very young. Pookie was a rabbit who could fly!

Why did you write this book?

I love plotting funny stories that are set in schools. They're my top things to write.

Is there anything in this book that relates to your own experiences?

I used to be a primary school teacher, and I have met many children like Harry, Nazreen, Krish and Lily!

What do you hope readers will get out of the book?

I hope the story makes readers laugh, but I also hope it makes them think.

Did you ever do any pranks at school?

No, I was a very well-behaved student. I did when I was a teacher though! On the last day of term, some teachers and I sneaked into the headteacher's office. Then we turned all the furniture around to face the wall!

Is the school in this story based on a school you know?

Not really, but it's a mix of many schools that I've worked in over the years.

Which of the characters in this story do you think you are most like? Why?

I think I would choose Nazreen because I'm quite bossy (just like she is!).

About the illustrator

What made you want to be an illustrator?

As a kid, I already loved creating my own characters and imaginary worlds. Giving life to stories and ideas became my passion and I found that illustration made it possible.

Paula Zorite

What did you like best about illustrating this book?

I specially loved illustrating the main characters. They have a lot of personality and interact in a very fun way with each other.

What was the most difficult thing about illustrating this book?

Working in different projects at the same time and dealing with all the deadlines can be challenging.

Is there anything in this book that relates to your own experiences?

When I was at school, my friends and I always loved to have little adventures during breaktime. Of course, playing detective was the best!

How do you bring a character to life in an illustration?

First, I think about the character's personality, age and environment. From this I create a general body structure. Then I go into details like the type of clothes they would be wearing, their hairstyles, facial expression ... until the character's appearance speaks for itself.

Do you ever base the characters you draw on people you know in real life?

Not intentionally, but I'm sure that subconsciously all the people that I have met and seen in my life influence the way I create certain characters.

Which character or scene did you most like illustrating?

I specially enjoyed illustrating the scene in which the characters can't hear Nazreen because of the bell. It's a funny scene and it came out being quite dynamic. I like that you can almost hear the extreme noise.

Did you ever pull any pranks when you were at school?

Not really. I've always been more into jokes than actual pranks. I was a very well-behaved kid and I guess I was worried about the possibility of hurting someone's feelings, even if the prank itself had very innocent intentions.

Book chat

Who was your favourite character, and why?

What did you think of the book at the start? Did you change your mind at all as you read it?

Which scene in this book stands out most for you? Why?

Were you surprised when you found out who had made the mess? Why, or why not?

Would you like to read another book about the same characters? If so, what might happen in it?

Who did you suspect as you read the book? Did you change your mind?

If you had to give the book a new title, what would you choose?

If you could talk to one character from the book, who would you pick? What would you say to them?

Did this book remind you of anything you have experienced in real life?

Book challenge:

Make fingerprints and compare them with someone else's.

Collins
BIG CAT

Published by Collins
An imprint of HarperCollins*Publishers*

The News Building
1 London Bridge Street
London SE1 9GF
UK

Macken House
39/40 Mayor Street Upper
Dublin 1
D01 C9W8
Ireland

ISBN 978-0-00-862462-0

Download the teaching notes and word cards to accompany this book at:
http://littlewandle.org.uk/signupfluency/

Get the latest Collins Big Cat news at
collins.co.uk/collinsbigcat

Author: Narinder Dhami
Illustrator: Paula Zorite (Advocate Art)
Publisher: Lizzie Catford
Product manager: Caroline Green
Series editor: Charlotte Raby
Development editor: Catherine Baker
Commissioning editor: Suzannah Ditchburn
Project manager: Emily Hooton
Content editor: Daniela Mora Chavarría
Phonics reviewer: Rachel Russ
Copyeditor: Catherine Dakin
Proofreader: Gaynor Spry
Typesetter: 2Hoots Publishing Services Ltd
Cover designer: Sarah Finan
Production controller: Katharine Willard

Printed and bound in the UK using 100% Renewable Electricity at Martins the Printers Ltd

Collins would like to thank the teachers and children at the following schools who took part in the trialling of Big Cat for Little Wandle Fluency: Burley And Woodhead Church of England Primary School; Chesterton Primary School; Lady Margaret Primary School; Little Sutton Primary School; Parsloes Primary School.

MIX
Paper | Supporting responsible forestry
FSC
www.fsc.org
FSC™ C007454